"BLISTERING HONESTY"

MEHAK JAIN

I'm thankful to all those people who have contributed in the successful completion of this book and would love to dedicate this book to all those who have played a part in this book.

Contents

Preface — vii

Acknowledgements — ix

About The Author — xi

1. Dear Mom — 1

2. I Don't Recognize You — 2

3. Disguised As A Sister — 3

4. The Games That You Play — 5

5. Dear Cuzz — 7

6. Circumstancial Friend — 8

7. Unknown You Were — 10

8. Sky Is The Limit — 12

9. Sterile Solace — 13

10. Perpetual Connection — 15

11. Perjurious Malice — 17

12. Reminiscences — 19

13. Dear Entity — 21

14. Separated But Still Together — 23

15. Dear Orthodoxy — 25

16. Miles Apart — 27

17. Dear God — 29

18. Vigorous You Have To Be — 31

19. Dear Brat — 33

20. Guide For A Reason — 35

21. Old Good Times — 37

Contents

22. Rotten But Remains 39

23. Naïve Times 41

24. You Gave Me Wings 43

25. Quick-witted You Are. 45

26. Incessant Need 47

27. You Made Me Stronger 49

28. Ambition Keeps Me Alive 51

29. Chaser 53

30. Dear Admirer 55

31. Dear Self 57

32. Second Mother To The Other 59

33. Dear Ungrudging 61

34. Strangers We Have Become 63

35. Dear Love 65

36. Mother Nature 67

37. Flutter To Flit 69

38. I Fly Because Of You 71

39. Parted Ways 73

40. Dear Unacquainted 75

Preface

The book consists of several poems that are designated to the poet's near and dear ones and some even deal with issues ongoing and highly prevalent in the society albeit the fact that they are not addressed directly but by signaling and holding onto people who are responsible for them.

Acknowledgements

I would like to thank poetic souls publication for giving me and many such writers like me the chance to grow as an individual and publish their own individual book. Then I would like to thank all my family and friends for being there with me and helping me throughout.

About The Author

Mehak Jain is a very ecstatic person when it comes to writing and reading. Her writings revolve around her beliefs and ideas and the way she looks at things, also she tries her level best to understand and inculcate the understandings and views of others around her too. She is a sedulous person in her field of interest and a keen observer of things around.

ONE
Dear Mom

Dear Mommy,
I start with you because you started me
I began with you because your new phase of life began with me
I complete you because you complete me.
There were times when I admired you but today,
I don't even recognize you
You and I have drifted apart,
You were my confidant but now I can't.
I tried really hard but couldn't make it end to the last.
Now, I don't even see your door a little ajar.
Mine is wide open,
For only you it has been kept open.
I know you love me,
But sometimes it must be expressed too.
I miss you,
But do you?

TWO

I DON'T RECOGNIZE YOU

•♡•

Dear Daddy,
I don't know why you don't express,
But this always makes me restless.
It hurts because you look distant,
Close to your files but far away from your homely life.
Piles of work you have and
Miles away we get.
Rarely do you speak but even then it seems meek.
You are clever because,
You never cared.
You seem like a good dad
But you never actually played that part.
You became a dad
But never accepted that fact.
You are cordial with everybody,
But with me, you tend to change.
Maybe I lack something,
Or is it just you being you?
Thank you.

THREE

DISGUISED AS A SISTER

Dear Sister,
Sweet at times,
But rough all the time.
You change colours more,
Than a chameleon.
You are younger than me,
But always want an upper hand on me.
You lie in my face,
And talk about trust on my face.
Nobody finds any of your mischiefs,
Because at it you are a chief.
Mind- washing is your thing,
And you make use of it when in need.
Exceptionally well you are in fooling,
Maybe that's why you are ruling.
I don't see why only I get scolded,
Maybe you are too good at moulding.
Sometimes I try,
But later I feel why?

“BLISTERING HONESTY”

Thank you.

FOUR

THE GAMES THAT YOU PLAY

Dear relatives,
I feel glad when I see you,
But when I hear you,
I don't feel the same thing for you.
You are good on the face but,
Pathetic behind,
And what more do I remind.
The memories I have are countless,
Lesser without fuss,
But most with cuss.
Your actions depict hypocrisy,
And then you practice autocracy.
You talk behind my back but,
Behave like you the only well-wisher that I can have.
I used to like your company,
But now I know why you accompanied,
Just to fulfil your purpose,
And to complete your circus.
But mind you, I'm better at your games.

"BLISTERING HONESTY"

Thank you.

FIVE
DEAR CUZZ

Dear cousins,
Having you is a blessing,
Until it became too assessing.
Childhood was fun,
When we all were one.
We have hundreds of memories,
Where we even shared our accessories.
Played thousands of games,
But now we call each other names.
We all tried somewhere,
But it didn't bring us anywhere.
Small, little things are now considered,
Because of which everything needs to be reconsidered.
I don't know why we have grown apart,
But you all still have my heart.
I'll try to mend this bond,
I just need you to respond.
That's all I can say from my heart.
Thank you.

SIX

CIRCUMSTANCIAL FRIEND

Dear friend,
I have you,
Because I have to,
I'm too shy,
To bash you.
I want us happening,
But you make it too difficult.
You twist words,
And work in herds.
Unreliable you are,
That's why we are this far.
You change your stance,
In a glance.
Everything you do,
Seems blue.
Still we are together,
Because you are clever.
You never miss a chance,
Like my aunts.

Thank you.

SEVEN

Unknown You Were

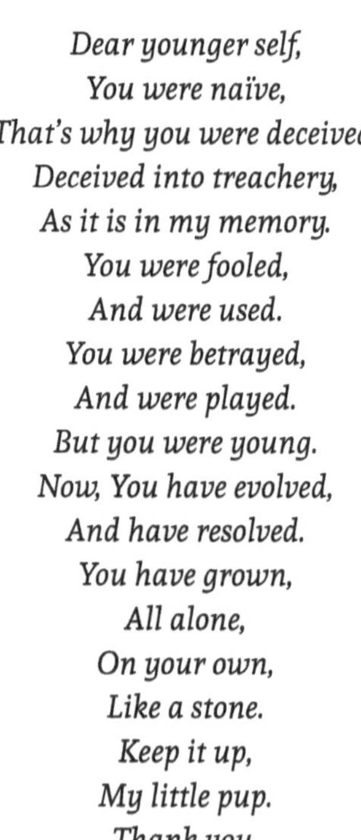

Dear younger self,
You were naïve,
That's why you were deceived.
Deceived into treachery,
As it is in my memory.
You were fooled,
And were used.
You were betrayed,
And were played.
But you were young.
Now, You have evolved,
And have resolved.
You have grown,
All alone,
On your own,
Like a stone.
Keep it up,
My little pup.
Thank you.

EIGHT

SKY IS THE LIMIT

Dear older self,
I see you,
Through,
With a view,
And like that,
You grew.
I see you,
Achieving something new,
And being true,
That though I always knew.
Though some things are always due,
But still, you pursue,
And flew,
And never withdrew.
You always renew,
And become anew,
Out of the dew,
And the taboo.
Like that you grew.
Thank you.

NINE
STERILE SOLACE

Dear beloved,
You claim to love me,
But I can't see,
And, I don't agree,
With thee.
I have been betrayed,
And played,
Because of this,
I'm afraid.
I stayed,
And obeyed,
Your opinion still swayed,
And like that,
The love decayed.
I was mislaid,
And forbade,
Still, I prayed,
But nothing stayed.
But you still claim to love me.
Now you tell me,
How do I behave?

“BLISTERING HONESTY”

Thank you.

• 14 •

TEN

PERPETUAL CONNECTION

Dear school life,
I miss you,
Every few.
It feels that something is due,
But I grew.
You taught me to pursue,
And to flew.
I renewed,
I construed,
Because of you.
You are a vital part,
Of my heart,
From the start,
But it was hard,
To depart,
And restart.
You define me,
In my degrees,
And I'm a devotee,

Of thee.
Thank you.

ELEVEN

PERJURIOUS MALICE

Dear classmates,
You all are sweet,
But let me complete,
You always compete,
And cheat,
And deceit.
You good on the face,
But always want to race,
And ace,
But you don't embrace,
Other's traits.
You too precocious,
And extremely ambitious.
Whim-inspired fool,
You are cruel,
And always drool,
So, you all must be in,
Preschools, pooled.
You fools.

“BLISTERING HONESTY”

Thank you.

TWELVE
REMINISCENCES

❦

Dear college life,
I miss the days,
And the ways,
All the delays,
And the stays.
This was a phase,
Of the plays,
And the essays,
With that craze.
Everything about you,
Seems anew,
Remembering you,
Is my accrue.
The best time it was,
You are the cause.
Of this art.
I feel you,
Every hour,
And feel prouder,
With every passing hour.
Thank you.

THIRTEEN
DEAR ENTITY

Dear life,
You have thousands of shades,
Which you made,
And displayed,
Every decade.
Every colour seems new,
In my view,
As you threw,
I grew.
You spare no one,
None,
And whoever trusted you,
Has won.
Once done,
You can't be redone,
For anyone.
One has to value you,
Because you come to few,
See the Jews.
Thank you.

FOURTEEN

SEPARATED BUT STILL TOGETHER

Dear ex,
I miss you,
Because I became accrue,
Of only you.
You have made me anew,
Because I askew,
Away from you.
You blew it,
When I had no clue about it.
But no matter what,
I would always do you,
Because still, something is due,
And I am glued.
Everything was new,
When I was with you,
But you were like them too,
Never true.
You screwed,
And I withdrew.

Thank you.

FIFTEEN

DEAR ORTHODOXY

Dear society,
You are biased,
And never are compliant,
You are not reliant,
In the lightest.
You have been untrue,
And there's nothing new,
Because we have been through,
To be true.
I never knew,
That you would view,
We girls as jews,
And out of blue.
But we never withdrew,
And will pursue,
And one day will blew,
This taboo,
And that day we subdue,
This slew,

And will make them ensue.
Thank you.

SIXTEEN
MILES APART

Dear long-distance friend,
We are miles apart,
But still together by heart,
Because you played a part,
At the start.
When times differed,
And we flickered,
Nothing was embittered,
And nothing was a blizzard.
Those were the times,
Which I remember sometimes,
When we had limes,
And felt primes,
Playing with slimes,
And chanting rhymes.
No lines,
No defines,
No whines,
No confines,
And only consigns.
Thank you.

SEVENTEEN
DEAR GOD

Dear God,
I feel blessed,
Because I have got the best.
You keep taking my test,
Because I have a quest,
To attest.
I just have a request,
In my chest,
Which is pressed,
To be possessed.
I want to contest,
And invest,
My rest.
This is all I ask of you,
Because I want to become accrue,
And anew,
And become askew,
Towards you.
Everything expressed,
Now you only suggest.
Thank you

EIGHTEEN

VIGOROUS YOU HAVE TO BE

Dear girl,
Your life is full of struggles,
And troubles,
Because society always chuckles,
But nobody cuddles.
You will have to solve puzzles,
Pass many dark tunnels,
And funnels,
To get rid of these fuckers.
You have to stay strong,
For long,
Because no one is along,
And nowhere you belong.
People will consider you wrong,
For prolong,
So thereon,
Be no one's pawn.
You are on your own,
And alone,

So, become like a stone,
And be your backbone.
Thank you.

• 32 •

NINETEEN
DEAR BRAT

Dear boy,
This society won't spare you,
Because they accrue,
Of you.
They are askew,
To you,
And this never construes.
This addiction is timeless,
Which makes you spineless,
And lifeless,
Because you are sightless,
Of the primeness.
You are the highness,
Though you are mindless,
You won't understand fineness,
As you only excel in slyness.
You need to change,
Or rearrange,
Otherwise, it will be strange,
And out of your range.
Thank you.

TWENTY

GUIDE FOR A REASON

Dear books,
You taught me so much,
Before,
Never experienced anything like such.
I was entangled in a clutch,
And caged in a hutch,
But when we came in touch,
I was deeply touched.
Your bunch,
Makes me skip my lunch.
I am clutched to you,
And have become accrue.
I forget to chew,
When I have you,
Because you only construe,
And I am glued.
I grew,
And became anew.
You are the reason,

Why I can't be weakened.
Thank you.

TWENTY-ONE
OLD GOOD TIMES

Dear old good memories,
Every day,
I pray,
That you stay,
And never go away,
Only today,
I say.
You display,
A ray,
And way,
Told they.
I cherish those plays,
And the clays,
When times were gay.
I want to delay,
Your decay,
Because hey,
You convey,
And portray,
Those old good days.
Thank you.

TWENTY-TWO

ROTTEN BUT REMAINS

Dear bad memories,
You are like a shadow,
That foreshadows,
And make me shallow.
You are like tobacco,
Making me narrow,
Like an arrow.
Nobody can know,
How you shadowed.
You play with brains,
And replay the remains,
That contains,
Several strains.
No gains,
And only pains,
That explains,
Your reins.
Your reigns,
Always pertains,

And never abstains.
Thank you.

TWENTY-THREE
NAÏVE TIMES

Dear childhood memories,
You are the best part of my life,
When there were no strifes,
And we lived our lives.
Nothing applied,
And nobody died,
And everything was just fine.
No files,
No drives,
Nothing to describe.
No devices,
No advices.
No defines,
No declines,
And everything was bright.
Then we were truly alive,
When nothing was denied,
And everything was in line.
Nothing to hide,
Or divide,
And when none had a disguise.

“BLISTERING HONESTY”

Thank you.

TWENTY-FOUR

YOU GAVE ME WINGS

Dear fairy tales,
You taught me to dream,
And be a team,
And never scheme.
I dreamed,
And beamed,
Even gleamed.
You taught me to fly,
Real high,
And that's how I learned to try.
You played a pivotal part,
Everything apart,
And stayed in my heart,
From the start.
You are close to me,
Beyond any degree,
And that's why,
I'm a devotee,
And a trustee,

Of thee.
Thank you.

TWENTY-FIVE

QUICK-WITTED YOU ARE.

Dear college mate,
You are smart,
From the start.
You mould things,
And spins,
Like swings.
You are clever,
Since forever.
You play with words,
And work in herds.
You dismay nerds,
Always work on your terms.
You are always in disguise,
That is witnessed by my eyes,
And you rise,
Only through lies.
You never fail to surprise,
With your replies,
Which are carefully devised.

And that's the reason for my despise.
Thank you.

TWENTY-SIX
INCESSANT NEED

Dear wishes,
You are never-ending,
Because of which I'm ever spending.
I'm ever depending,
And something is always pending.
You are always extending,
And never descending.
Everything new is trending,
And therefore the list becomes unending.
I'm spending,
And fending.
This poem is representing,
Wishes that are unrelenting,
And girls,
Those can't be prevented.
I'm one of you,
Because I accrue,
To every anew.
Though I try to ensue,
But it is still due.
Thank you.

TWENTY-SEVEN

YOU MADE ME STRONGER

Dear breakdowns,
You break me apart,
And my heart,
Into many parts,
That's your art.
From the start,
You never depart,
Though I want to restart.
I emerge stronger,
After every longueur,
And you seem smaller,
And I become the reconquer.
Every tear made me anew,
And the credit goes to you,
Because now I'm through,
To be true.
In my view,
I grew,
And became new,

Because of you.
Thank you.

TWENTY-EIGHT
AMBITION KEEPS ME ALIVE

Dear passion,
You act as fuel,
Because of which I get fuelled.
You are a jewel,
And we make a good dual,
Because you are a great refuel,
When days are cruel.
You are crucial,
And one of my jewels.
You instigate something in me,
Because of which I've reached a degree,
I'm a devotee,
Of only thee.
I've come this far,
When the doors were just ajar,
And dark was my scars.
I've grown,
And become known,
Because you never left me alone,

And on my own.
Thank you.

TWENTY-NINE
CHASER

Dear stalker,
You have messed up my peace,
And my anxiety increase,
But your actions never cease,
Or decrease.
You are geese,
And I want your gestures to surcease.
All streets,
Have you cheats,
With your increased,
New techniques.
Your presence makes me quiver,
And I shiver,
As it feels bitter,
And something triggers.
I can't be clearer,
That you are a sinner.
You are shameless,
And consider yourself blameless,
Though you are baseless.
Thank you.

THIRTY
DEAR ADMIRER

Dear admirer,
You make my day,
As they say,
It's the way,
You say,
My name.
We are away,
But only today,
And one day,
You will stay.
It's the way,
You lay,
And survey,
And display,
That ray,
Of gay.
I pray,
For you to be okay,
And hey,
You shall never decay,
So, please obey.

Thank you.

THIRTY-ONE
DEAR SELF

Dear self,
Your growth is remarkable,
And not at all hierarchical.
You don't need to stop,
You will reach the top.
There will be stops,
But you adopt.
Keep adapting,
And interacting.
Stop reacting,
Then only you become impacting.
You might collapse,
And perhaps,
That's how you rise from scraps.
There will be traps,
And several attacks,
Because they have hearts of black,
But you relax.
You will be fine,
And will always shine.
Thank you.

THIRTY-TWO

SECOND MOTHER TO THE OTHER

Dear teacher,
You are the second mother,
To the other.
You taught me to discover,
And to recover.
It's you who moulded me into this mould,
Though you were cold,
But you are gold.
You were bold,
And told me the road,
Which never closed,
But only glowed.
Being you is difficult,
Because your role is magnificent,
And munificent,
And you make it more significant.
You are incomparable,
And your dedication indomitable,
And thus you become honourable,

And memorable.
Thank you.

THIRTY-THREE
DEAR UNGRUDGING

Dear trees,
You are the true epitome of sacrifice,
Though we may not recite,
Because nothing had sufficed,
The thirst that always magnifies.
Your greatness has been talked about,
Centuries and throughout,
But I have a doubt,
Why do there still exist droughts?
There is no account,
And no amount,
With no count,
Of you ploughed.
Some of you are worshipped,
The rest are snipped,
And shipped.
You are a gift,
Because of which we exist,
We stay fit,

Because you exist.
Thank you.

THIRTY-FOUR

STRANGERS WE HAVE BECOME

Dear elder sister,
You were like a friend to me,
Because back then there was no perjury.
You changed with time,
And stated something sublime,
As crime.
Times change,
But you shouldn't have changed,
Something that was fine.
Us combined,
Was something divine,
To define.
Together we shined,
Always aligned,
And inclined,
But never confined.
You changed sides,
And created these divides,
Though we matched vibes,

But those were some different times.
Thank you.

THIRTY-FIVE
DEAR LOVE

Dear love,
I tried to find you,
But you never construe.
You made me anew,
Out of the blue.
I had no clue,
And was in dew,
But it all ensued,
And I grew.
You come to few,
That's what I knew,
Or maybe I misconstrued.
You come to those,
Who keep you close,
And stay composed,
And never impose.
People say different things,
From kings,
To new springs,
But everybody sings,
The same hymns,

That you give wings.
Thank you.

THIRTY-SIX
MOTHER NATURE

Dear nature,
Your sacrifices are countless,
And boundless,
That is doubtless.
You surround us,
And are around us,
Because you are endless.
You have endowed us,
With this brown dust.
You are priceless,
And timeless,
Without you,
We are lifeless.
You are guileless,
That is your niceness,
And your absence,
Makes us spineless.
Without you we are guideless,
And our faces,
Smile less.
Thank you.

THIRTY-SEVEN
FLUTTER TO FLIT

Dear self,
You have seen so much,
Because the situation was such,
When no one was in touch,
And everyone remained untouched.
I have observed,
That you have emerged,
Because you never diverged,
And have learned,
To be like a bird.
Loyal you have remained,
That's why you have sustained,
And today you have gained,
Everything you named,
Because you have maintained,
And have trained.
From an egg you have become a bird,
Because you never worked in herd.
You were fooled,
And ruled,
Hence used.

People always assumed,
And misused,
But you proved,
That you can be improved,
And today you are approved,
And have renewed,
To conclude.
Thank you.

THIRTY-EIGHT

I FLY BECAUSE OF YOU

❧

Dear best friend,
You taught me,
What it is to be,
Like a bee.
Careless and carefree,
Like it, you set me free.
You my wings,
Because of which I feel like kings.
You give me strength,
That's why I've crossed this much length.
You know me in and out,
And I want you throughout.
This confidence that I wear,
Has been a gift from you dear.
I owe you,
And that is true.
So, just remember,
I value us,
More than any Gus.

Thank you.

THIRTY-NINE
PARTED WAYS

❥

Dear neighborhood friend,
We used to be so close,
Wearing each other's coats,
Making notes,
Or so it was called by most.
Exchanging jokes,
Fully engrossed,
Having so many hopes.
We were inseparable,
Our meetings were always pleasurable,
And preferable,
And now memorable.
We have separated our ways,
Forgetting those days,
And that phase,
Of so many stays.
This conveys,
That everything decays,
And portrays,
Many betrays.
Thank you.

FORTY

DEAR UNACQUAINTED

Dear strangers,
You stare at us,
And discuss,
Thus make a fuss.
Deprived of nous,
You drive us nuts.
But we have guts,
Which makes you shut.
We try to adjust,
Because it is a must,
But surely unjust,
Because it disgusts.
Your stares leave an impact,
And that is a fact,
Though we stay intact,
And never react,
But it's all tact.
In fact,
We enact,

And adapt,
Because we are trapped.
Thank you.

www.ingramcontent.com/pod-product-compliance
Lightning Source LLC
Chambersburg PA
CBHW061355160726
47995CB00001B/333